Contents

Words appearing in the text in bold, **like this**, are explained in the Glossary.

 Find out more about Brazil at www.heinemannexplore.co.uk

Where is Brazil?

To learn more about Brazil we meet three children who live there. Brazil is in South America. Brazil is the largest country in South America.

▲ This is a map of Brazil. The capital city of Brazil is Brasília.

Brazil has many **plains**, hills and mountains. The weather in Brazil is **tropical**. Brazil has a huge rainforest. The rainforest plants grow well in the tropical weather.

Most people in Brazil ▶ live in cities.

▼ The Amazon River and Rainforest cover most of north and central Brazil.

Meet Guilherme

Guilherme is six years old. He lives in Rio de Janeiro. Guilherme lives with his mother, father, sister and grandparents. His father is a **publisher**. His mother runs a nursery.

▼ Guilherme and his family like to go to the beach.

Guilherme's mother

Guilherme's father

Guilherme

Guilherme's sister

▼ Guilherme enjoys barbeques, but his favourite foods are prawns and cheese omelette!

Guilherme's family sometimes have a barbeque. Guilherme likes eating fish and steak cooked on the barbeque.

Guilherme's day

Guilherme goes to school five days a week. There are 20 children in his class. He is taught maths, English, art, Portuguese and religion. Guilherme likes learning English.

▲ Guilherme's school is nearby so he can walk there.

Guilherme's grandmother

At break Guilherme and his friends play football in the playground. When he gets home from school, Guilherme has to do an hour of homework.

9

Fun in Rio

Guilherme loves swimming and football. He lives near a very famous football stadium called the Maracanã. Guilherme wants to be a swimming teacher when he grows up.

◀ Guilherme supports Brazil's football team.

◀ The most famous Carnaval celebration is in Rio de Janeiro.

A big celebration takes place in February, called Carnaval. Guilherme enjoys Carnaval! There are parades through the streets. People dress up and dance to **samba** music.

11

Football

Many Brazilian people love football. They call it futebol. Brazil's football team is very famous. They are the first team to have won the World Cup five times.

▲ People everywhere enjoy playing and watching football.

▼ Pelé played in the Maracanã
   Stadium in Rio de Janeiro.

Pelé is known as one of the world's
best ever football players. He is from
Brazil. He played for football teams
between 1956 and 1977. He scored
more than 1200 goals!

Meet Christian

Christian is seven years old. He lives in a village in Minas Gerais. Christian lives with his mother and father. Their village is small and everyone knows each other.

▼ Christian's grandparents live next door.

Christian's mother

Christian's grandparents

Christian

Christian's father

Christian's house has a garden and a cornfield where he can play. Lots of Christian's family live near him. He likes to visit them.

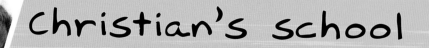

Christian's school

Christian walks to school with his cousins. Christian has lots of good friends at school. His best friends are Edgar and Tonineo.

▲ Christian lives near his school, so he can walk there.

Christian's teacher

▼ Christian and his friends enjoy going to school.

There are 20 children in Christian's class. They learn maths, geography, Portuguese, history, science and religion. Christian's favourite subject is science.

17

At home

After school, Christian does his homework. Christian's mother and father both work at home. Christian's father makes bowls out of **soapstone**.

▼ When Christian grows up, he would like to make bowls too.

▼ Christian's mother **weaves** rugs in their home.

Christian's mother makes rugs. She
sells them in the village. The family
also grow most of the food they eat.

Landmarks

Brazil is a beautiful country with landmarks to see. There are some huge waterfalls called the Iguaçu Falls. They are over three kilometres (two miles) wide!

▲ Many tourists visit these beautiful waterfalls.

This is the view from the top ▶
of Sugar Loaf Mountain.

Another famous place in Brazil is
Sugar Loaf Mountain. It has a statue
of Jesus on top. Tourists can go up the
mountain in a **cable car**.

Meet Ingrid

Ingrid is eight years old. She lives in Amazonia with her mother, father, brothers and sister. They spend a lot of time outside. They work or play near the house.

Ingrid's mother

Ingrid's father

Ingrid's sister

Ingrid

Ingrid's brothers

▲ Ingrid's house is made of wood.

▼ Ingrid likes playing outside in the rain.

Amazonia is the area of land around the Amazon River. The weather there is very warm and rainy. Ingrid's village is a safe place to live, although there are many snakes!

Working hard

Ingrid helps her mother and father with their work. Ingrid's mother works in the house. Ingrid helps her mother with her housework. She helps her by laying the table for meals.

Ingrid helps to wash the ▶ family's clothes too.

▼ Ingrid enjoys watching her father get ready to go fishing.

Ingrid's father is a fisherman. He brings fish home for the family to eat. Sometimes Ingrid helps him on the boat.

School and play

Ingrid goes to school for five days a week. She enjoys learning Portuguese, but she does not like history! Ingrid wants to be a doctor when she grows up.

▲ After school, Ingrid does her homework for half an hour.

When Ingrid has free time, she likes to play with her friend Alime. Ingrid also likes to go out on her bike around the village.

Nature and wildlife

A lot of Brazil is covered in **rainforest**. There is rainforest all along the Amazon River. Many **rare** plants and animals live there.

▼ Brazil has many unusual trees and plants.

Many of the plants and animals in Amazonia are in danger. Large parts of the rainforest are being destroyed. Some people want to clear the land for farming or to sell the trees as **timber**.

Over 18,000 types ▶ of animal live in Amazonia!

Brazilian fact file

Flag

Capital city

Money

Brazilia

Real

Religion
• Around 80 percent of people in Brazil are Roman Catholic Christians.

Language
• Portuguese is the official language of Brazil, but people also speak Spanish, English and French.

Try speaking Portuguese!
Olá .... Hello.
Cuidado .... Take care.
Muito obrigado / obrigada .... Thank you very much.

 Find out more about Brazil at
www.heinemannexplore.co.uk

Glossary

cable car small room that moves along an overhead cable to take people up and down mountains

plain large, flat, grassy area of land with few trees

publisher someone who makes books

samba Brazilian dance

soapstone type of rock, often used to make pots of ornaments

rainforest thick forest of tall trees that grows in a hot, rainy place

rare something that there are not many of

tropical hot and muggy, with lots of rain

timber wood that is ready for building work

weave way of knitting together threads to make a rug

More books to read

Continents: South America, Mary Virginia Fox (Heinemann Library, 2002)

Rainforest explorer, Greg Pyers (Raintree, 2004)

The Vanishing Rainforest, Richard Platt and Rupert Van Wyk, (Frances Lincoln Ltd, 2003)

Index